Okay,
Good Dog

by Ursula Landshoff

An I CAN READ Book

about training your dog

Harper & Row, Publishers

New York, Hagerstown, San Francisco, London

FIRST EDITION

Library of Congress Cataloging in Publication Data
Landshoff, Ursula.
    Okay, Good Dog.

    (An I can read book)
    SUMMARY: Presents simple instructions for training a dog.
    1. Dogs—Training—Juvenile literature.   [1. Dogs—Training]   I. Title.
SF431.L365   636.7'08'87   77-25648
ISBN 0-06-023672-8
ISBN 0-06-023673-6 lib. bdg.

Okay, Good Dog

To my coauthor, Doodles

CONTENTS

DO YOU WANT A DOG?

Do you want to own a dog?

Do you know a dog needs training?

If you want a dog,

you should train it yourself.

A dog can be your best friend.

If you want a dog,

you must ask yourself:

Do I want a big dog

or a small dog?

A male dog

or a female dog?

Do I want a dog with short hair?

Or with long hair?

You must brush your dog's hair.

You must wash him

and keep him clean.

There are many kinds of dogs.

They are called breeds.

All breeds are trained the same way.

11

There are many places to get dogs.

When you go to pick out your dog,

look at the dogs for a long time.

Pick one that is lively and nosy.

Pick one you love.

He will love you right back.

It is good to take your dog
to an animal doctor right away.
The doctor will check your dog
and give him shots
to make sure he stays healthy.

Take your dog home.

Introduce him to your family.

Give him a name.

Your dog will be shy at first.

He misses his mother

and the other dogs.

Do not let your friends

scare him with noisy noises.

Put him in a small pen by himself.

Put old newspapers on the floor.

Leave a dish with water

near him all the time.

A tick-tock clock will help

to keep him quiet.

If it is cool,

give him a small blanket.

A puppy needs to be warm.

Feed him

and wish him happy dreams.

HOUSEBREAKING YOUR DOG

Next morning the paper will be wet.

Throw the paper away.

Put new papers on the floor.

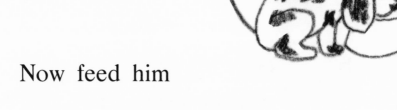

Now feed him

and let him eat quietly.

Feed him at the same time every day.

If your dog gobbles his food,

this means he is healthy.

A healthy dog is a happy dog.

Dogs must have a lot of exercise

Play with him.

A tennis ball is a very good toy.

Uh-oh.

Is he reading the newspaper?

No. He has used the newspaper

you put on the floor.

Paper training is the best way

to housebreak your dog.

Put a lot of paper

on the floor of his pen.

Change the paper

when it gets wet or dirty.

Before you let him out of his pen,

put paper on the floor.

Always put the paper

in the same places.

Watch him when he runs around.

If he squats where there is no paper,

quickly lift him up.

Put him on the paper

before he messes up the floor.

Soon he will learn

to go on the paper all by himself.

Whenever he wets or dirties the paper,

pet him and make a fuss over him.

Mistakes do happen.

Sometimes your dog

will not reach the paper in time.

Say "NO" in a loud voice.

But do not punish him.

Gradually take the paper

in his pen away.

Take your dog on a leash
early in his life.
It is safer to walk him
on the street with a leash.
In many cities, it is the law.
At first he may not like it.

But soon he will feel

it is his telephone to you.

Take him for a walk every day.

He will enjoy seeing

the world with you.

Stay out long enough for him to go.

He may still want to use some paper.

TEACH YOUR DOG TO SIT

When he is four months old,

you can teach your dog to sit.

Take him to a quiet place

where you are alone with him.

Push his backside down.

Say, "Sit" at the same time.

27

Keep saying "Sit."

Pet him when he does sit.

Say, "Good dog, sit."

Do not yell or scold

if your dog wants to play.

Say, "No" gently.

Show him how to sit

again and again.

28

When he gets up, say, "No."

Always try again.

Say, "Good dog, sit."

Your dog likes your attention.

Sometimes he may not feel

like a good dog.

He gets tired.

Or he sees something interesting.

Tempt him with a small piece
of dog biscuit.

31

Never, never hit your dog
with your hand.
Try this trick instead.
Roll up an old magazine
and hit the floor with it.
It makes a loud noise.
Your dog will pay attention.
Pet him. He will be quiet.

Always finish a lesson
after five minutes.
Start again later.

In a few days,
your dog will sit
without your hand
on his back.

33

At first he will sit

for only a short time.

When he sits,

say, "Okay, good dog."

And before he changes his mind,

stop the lesson.

Always stop a lesson
with a good performance.
That way you and your dog
will be happy.
You will look forward
to the next lesson.

TEACH YOUR DOG TO LIE DOWN

You can teach your dog to lie down.

First tell your dog to sit.

Then *gently* pull his front feet

out in front of him

until he is down.

Say, "Down" often.

36

Watch him.

If he wants to get up

put your hand

on his front shoulders.

Push down gently.

Remember, do not yell.

Praise him when he does
the right thing.

Teach him one thing at a time.

When he knows one trick well,
teach him a new one.

TEACH YOUR DOG TO COME

You can teach your dog to come.

Call your dog's name
and say, "Come."

Pull his leash gently to you
until he is right by your feet.
Now praise and pet your dog.

Here is an easy way
to teach your dog to come:
Ask a friend to help you.
Each person holds a treat
in his or her hand.
First your friend says, "Come...."
When your dog comes to your friend,
he gets the treat.

Then you say, "Come...."

When he comes to you,

you give him a treat.

Give him only small treats

so he does not get too fat.

Pet him and praise him

each time he comes to you.

Your dog will have so much fun

running between you two

that he will learn "come" easily.

There is one important thing to know.

Do not say, "Come" to your dog

when you want to punish him.

TEACH YOUR DOG TO HEEL

When your dog is six months old,
you should show him
how to "heel" on a leash.
To do this you need
a training collar.

Slip the collar

over the dog's neck.

The collar has two rings.

Snap the leash to the outside ring.

Pull the leash.

The collar will get tighter.

Do not pull hard.

You can hurt your dog if you do.

43

Have your dog stay
on your left side.
Hold the leash tight
in your right hand.

Give the leash a quick pull

with your left hand.

Let it loose quickly.

Do this until you have

your dog's attention.

Call your dog's name.

Say, "Heel," and start to walk.

Keep the leash short.

Keep your dog at your side.

If he goes out of step,

stop right away.

A puppy will pull the wrong way.

Sometimes he will sit down,

or walk in circles.

Don't yell at him.

Stop, and start again.

Each time you stop, say, "Halt."

Then say, "Heel," and walk again.

The leash should be loose.

Give it a quick pull

to correct your dog.

He should walk next to you.

He should not pull.

He should not drag behind.

Practice "heel" every day.

Practice indoors

between chairs and tables.

Practice outdoors, too.

Once your dog heels well,

change your step.

Walk slowly

and tell him, "Slow."

Walk fast,

and tell him, "Fast."

You can even run.

Your dog will love this best.

But always make sure

he stays at your side.

TEACH YOUR DOG TO STAY

To teach your dog to "stay,"

use a leash or rope

at least ten feet long.

Put the leash on your dog.

Tell him to lie down.

Hold the end of the leash

and stand at his side.

Say, "Stay."

Walk backward
away from him.

Keep watching him

while you say, "Stay."

Keep the leash in your hand.

When he tries to get up,

rush back to him.

Say, "NO, STAY."

If the dog tries to get up,

step on the leash.

This will keep him down.

Make him stay

a little longer each time.

Say, "Okay, good dog."

Pet him and praise him.

Then start over again.

When he can stay

for a minute or so,

walk away from him.

Keep the long leash in your hand.

Do not look at him.

Turn around after a few steps.

Soon you can let the leash

lie on the floor.

One day he will be able

to stay for ten minutes.

Then you can tell him, "Stay,"

and leave the room.

Watch from around the corner.

When he stays long enough,

go back to him,

pet him, and say, "Okay,

you are a very good dog."

Let him have a treat.

SOME TRICKS

To teach your dog to sit up,

make him sit in a corner

where he can lean

against the wall.

Say, "Sit up."

Lift his front feet up.

Push his back gently
against the wall
until he sits straight.

Say, "Sit up" again.
Next, hold a treat high
over his head,
and say, "Sit up."
He will soon do it all by himself.

To teach your dog

to jump through a hoop,

make him sit and stay.

Walk away a few steps.

Hold a hoop near the floor.

Make sure your dog

has to jump through the hoop

and cannot circle around it.

Hold the hoop with one hand

and have a reward ready

in the other hand.

Call him and say, "Jump."

He will love to jump to the reward.

When the dog knows how
to jump through the hoop,
you can raise the hoop.
Raise it a little each time.
Make sure the floor
is not slippery.

SOME ADVICE

Sometimes you want to take

your dog in the car with you.

But dogs can get carsick.

Take a roll of paper towels

to clean up

in case your dog *does* get sick.

When your dog starts to drool,

stop the car.

Take him out on the leash

to get fresh air.

Let him feel the ground

under his feet.

Walk him a few steps.

Then get back into the car.

Each time your dog drools,

stop the car.

Take him out in the fresh air

for a few minutes.

After three or four rides

he will look forward

to drives in the car.

It is better to stop your dog

from doing bad things

before he gets bad habits.

Say, "NO" when you see him

do something he should not do.

When your dog does

something right,

pet him and praise him.

Play with him.

Give him love.

A happy dog will be

your best friend for a long time.